Things You Didn't Know About Your **Body**

John Townsend

Chicago, Illinois

www.heinemannraintree.com
Visit our website to find out more information about Heinemann-Raintree books.

To order:
☎ Phone 888-454-2279
▣ Visit www.heinemannraintree.com to browse our catalog and order online.

Edited by Andrew Farrow and Adam Miller
Designed by Richard Parker
Picture research by Ruth Blair
Originated by Capstone Global Library Ltd
Printed and bound in China by South China Printing Company Ltd

15 14 13 12 11
10 9 8 7 6 5 4 3 2 1

Library of Congress Cataloging-in-Publication Data
Townsend, John, 1955–
101 things you didn't know about your body / John Townsend.
    p. cm.—(101)
Includes bibliographical references and index.
ISBN 978-1-4109-3896-1 (hc) -- ISBN 978-1-4109-4383-5 (pb)
1. Human body—Juvenile literature. 2. Human physiology—Juvenile literature. 3. Teenagers—Health and hygiene—Juvenile literature. I. Title. II. Title: One hundred and one things you didn't know about your body. III. Title: One hundred one things you didn't know about your body.
QP37.T594 2011
612—dc22   2010033915

Acknowledgments
We would like to thank the following for permission to reproduce photographs: Alamy pp (imagebroker), **12** (Chris Rout); Bridgeman Art Library p **27** (Private Collection/Archives Charmet); Corbis pp **5** (Patrik Giardino), **6** (Dr David Phillips/Visuals Unlimited), **9** (Rick Gomez), **13** (Patrik Giardino), **16** (Jack Hollingsworth), **21** (Patrik Giardino), **33** (Dennis Kunkel Microscopy, Inc./Visuals Unlimited), **35** (Stephane Reix/For Picture), **37** (Thom Lang), **39** (Rainer Holz), **40** (Image Source), **46** (Helen King), **47** (Eric Cahan); Getty Images p **15** (Fred Duval/FilmMagic); iStockphoto pp **19** (Berit Skogmo), **22** (Haykirdi), **23** (Sharon Dominick), **43 left** (Daniel Bobrowsky), **43 right** (Devon Gustin), **45** (Sharon Meredith), **48** (Greg Epperson); Science Photo Library pp **11 bottom** (Gastrolab), **20** (CNRI), **31** (US National Library Of Medicine), Shutterstock pp **7** (carroteater), **11 top** (Mikael Damkier), **17** (Sebastian Kaulitzki), **26** (Henri Schmit), **29** (Marilyn Barbone), **32** (Sebastian Kaulitzki).

Cover photograph of a girl, airborne, with a basketball reproduced with permission of Getty Images (Ron Levine).

Every effort has been made to contact copyright holders of any material reproduced in this book. Any omissions will be rectified in subsequent printings if notice is given to the publisher.

Disclaimer
All the Internet addresses (URLs) given in this book were valid at the time of going to press. However, due to the dynamic nature of the Internet, some addresses may have changed, or sites may have changed or ceased to exist since publication. While the author and publisher regret any inconvenience this may cause readers, no responsibility for any such changes can be accepted by either the author or the publisher.

Contents

J
619
J664

Words appearing in the text in bold, **like this**, are explained
in the Glossary.

Your Body Up Close

You are amazing! Your body is an incredible machine full of surprises. You are about to find out some of its secrets, and the answers to such weird questions as:

- Why doesn't my belly button heal up?
- Will my hair keep growing after I die?
- Do I shrink during the day?

One bizarre question some people ask is: "How much is my body worth?" Believe it or not, someone tried to figure out the answer. The U.S. Bureau of Chemistry and Soils figured out that all the parts of the human body put together are worth about $4.50!

You are made of:
- 65% oxygen
- 18% carbon (enough to make 900 pencils)
- 10% hydrogen
- 3% nitrogen
- 1.5% calcium
- 1% phosphorous (enough to make 2,200 match heads)
- 0.35% potassium
- 0.25% sulfur (enough to kill the fleas on an average-size dog)
- 0.15% sodium
- 0.15% chlorine
- 0.6% other

01 Your body has tiny amounts of magnesium, iron, manganese, zinc, copper, aluminum, and even arsenic. You contain many gallons of water, as well as enough fat to make about seven bars of soap. Your body is made up of trillions of tiny building blocks—your cells.

02 The adult body is made up of trillions of cells. There are many different kinds, such as muscle cells, bone cells, nerve cells, and blood cells. Over time they wear out and die, so your body is replacing them all the time. Your cells divide and make new cells, but you don't even notice. In fact, your body creates a billion new cells every minute!

But there's more. . . . What holds this amazing body of yours together and stops you from falling apart on the floor?

03 Your bones hold you up. You were born with over 300 bones, but as you grow many of these bones join together. By the time you are an adult, you will have 206 bones. Twenty-seven of those are in your hand and fourteen are in your face. The longest bone in your body is your thighbone, the femur, which is about a quarter of your height. Your smallest bone is the stirrup bone in your ear, which is only 2.5 millimeters (0.09 inches) long.

04 Your skin holds you together and is your biggest organ. An adult's skin is about the size of a blanket. Skin cells are constantly shedding and being replaced. In fact, you are likely to shed almost 20 kilograms (44 pounds) of skin in your lifetime.

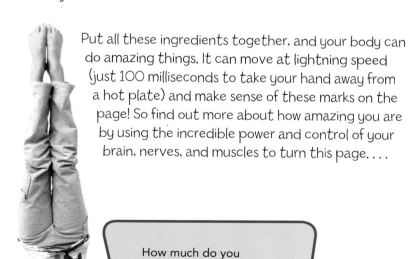

Put all these ingredients together, and your body can do amazing things. It can move at lightning speed (just 100 milliseconds to take your hand away from a hot plate) and make sense of these marks on the page! So find out more about how amazing you are by using the incredible power and control of your brain, nerves, and muscles to turn this page. . . .

How much do you really know about all your amazing parts?

Body Secrets

Get ready to be shocked. Your body is home to all sorts of tiny creatures. You are never really completely alone!

05 Scientists believe there are more **bacteria** in your body than the total number of your cells. There are billions of bacteria on each of your feet alone. You are crawling with life!

What's that?

Bacteria are simple, single-celled organisms that exist either alone or in colonies. Even though we cannot see bacteria, we interact with trillions of them every day.

06 People often think of bacteria as germs that can get into our bodies and make us sick. This is partly true, as some bacteria can be dangerous. However, many bacteria do not harm us at all. Scientists have discovered that certain kinds of bacteria are essential for the human body to stay healthy. They think many of the bacteria on your body right now are important for keeping your skin healthy.

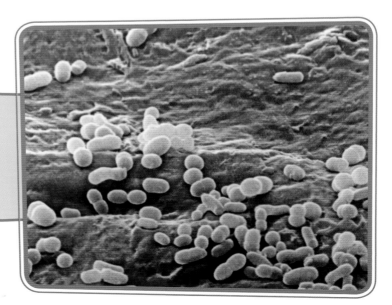

This is what the bacteria on your skin look like when seen under a microscope.

Our little friends

In 2009 scientists from the National Human Genome Research Institute in Bethesda, Maryland, carried out an experiment. They asked volunteers to wash with soap for one week, before going 24 hours without washing at all. Then the volunteers arrived at the laboratory to have their bodies swabbed. The scientists found about 1,000 different species of bacteria on each person. The study's results showed that "microbes that live in and on our bodies outnumber our own cells by ten to one."

07 Good bacteria in your intestines help you to digest food, keep out the bad bacteria, and get rid of **toxins** in your body. Good bacteria improve your tolerance to milk, help you to avoid food allergies and diarrhea, improve your **immune** system, help regulate blood pressure, and lower the **cholesterol** in your blood. No wonder they're called friendly bacteria.

08 Athlete's foot is a type of fungus that can infect skin between the toes, under toenails, and around the sides of the feet. The itchy fungi thrive in warm, moist places. They can be easily treated with anti-fungal cream, spray, or powder. Fungi are **parasites** because they are organisms that live on other living things.

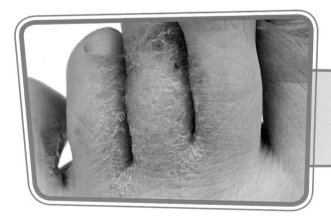

Athlete's foot fungus often spreads on sweaty or damp feet.

Right now there are over one million dust mites on your mattress and pillow, munching the dead skin cells that fell off you last night! Such microscopic life is invisible to the naked eye.

listen up!

Body Invaders

Bad bacteria can attack your body in many ways and cause diseases. That's why keeping clean is so important. But you might be surprised to know where bacteria are at work right now—in your mouth! If there is some sugar in there, too, those bacteria will be having a party. Brace yourself for the next mind-boggling fact about your body. . . .

09 Your mouth contains more bacteria than the entire world's population!

> **"There are 100 million [bacteria] in every milliliter of saliva and more than 600 different species in the mouth."**
>
> —Professor William Wade, The Dental Institute at King's College, London, England

10 With all those bacteria in your mouth, it is hardly surprising that one of the most common diseases in the world today is tooth decay. This is caused by sticky deposits, called **plaque**, that collect around the gums and between the teeth. Plaque is made up of bits of food, saliva, and bacteria. In time, the acid in plaque can dissolve away the enamel coating on each tooth, making holes that destroy the nerve and blood vessels inside.

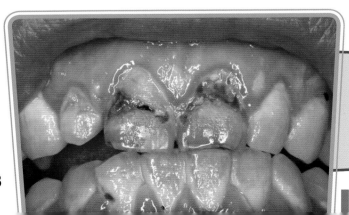

Before people knew about mouth bacteria, tooth decay like this was common.

More invaders

Unlike bacteria, viruses are body invaders that cannot live on their own. They need to be inside living cells to grow. Most viruses cannot survive very long outside a living cell. So far, scientists have identified only 4,000 different viruses, but they believe 400,000 types could exist on Earth.

Stop the decay! Brushing your teeth regularly keeps mouth bacteria at a healthy level.

11 The most common type of virus to affect humans is one of over 200 different types of cold virus. That is why we keep catching colds! Once your body has fought off a particular cold virus, you usually do not catch it again. The trouble is that viruses are very good at changing, or **mutating**. Flu (influenza) is a common human virus that mutates. These changes are usually small enough for our bodies to recognize parts of the virus and eventually fight it off. About every 10 years, a flu virus changes and causes more severe cases, and even **epidemics**.

12 A flu virus can survive up to 48 hours on surfaces such as door handles, desks, and keyboards. You can spread the flu virus to other people up to a day before you get symptoms, and three to seven days after symptoms start. So if you catch the flu, stay indoors, rest, and read a good book!

13 Your body is a constant battleground because it is always fighting invaders. Your amazing immune system deals with millions of bacteria and viruses each day to keep you healthy. Your cells produce chemicals called **antibodies** that attach themselves to a virus and work to destroy it.

Food for Thought

Your stomach is another amazing part of your body. It is a large bag of muscles that squeezes and churns by contracting and relaxing all the time. But that's not all. It has some scary chemicals inside it, too.

14 There is some very strong hydrochloric acid sloshing around inside your stomach. This acid kills bad bacteria and helps you to digest even the toughest pizza crust. The hydrochloric acid is even strong enough to dissolve many types of metal!

If I have powerful acid inside me, why doesn't my stomach dissolve and digest itself?

Your stomach is lined with a slimy coating called **mucus**. Every two weeks your stomach makes a new layer of mucus to stop the acid from eating into your stomach walls. Sometimes things can go wrong, and the acid burns through the mucus and starts a stomach **ulcer**. This can be treated with medication.

15 After your churned-up meal has sloshed around in your stomach for a while, it becomes a sloppy liquid. It is then pushed through to your small intestine, where more chemicals break it down even further. The small intestine soaks up the nutrients, which eventually flow into your bloodstream. The leftover sludge is pushed into your large intestine. There the moisture from your food is squeezed out and recycled back into your body.

16 An adult's stomach can hold about 1.5 liters (1.6 quarts) of churning food and liquid. Each day over 10 liters (10.6 quarts) of digested food, liquids, and digestive juices flow through your digestive system. As little as about 100 milliliters (3.4 fluid ounces) are **excreted** at the other end as **feces**.

17 It only takes a few seconds for food to go from your mouth to your stomach. But it takes your body around 12 hours to digest swallowed food completely. Even before it enters your stomach, chewed food has been soaked with saliva in your mouth. In fact, you produce on average over 500 milliliters (17 fluid ounces) of saliva a day. That's almost 20,000 liters (5,285 gallons) in a lifetime—a tanker load of saliva!

18 In your lifetime, your body will need a warehouse full of food and drink to keep it going. You will drink about 75,000 liters (19,800 gallons or almost four of those tankers) of water, and your digestive system may have to cope with about 45 tonnes (50 tons) of food. That's like eating six elephants! You'll excrete in solid waste the weight of one to two elephants! So where do you think the four remaining elephants go? They are burned up as energy, turned into heat, sweated out, and breathed out!

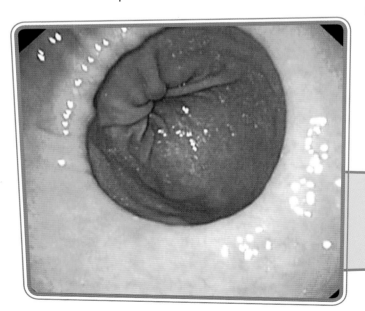

This is what a healthy stomach looks like.

Do I need fat?

Whatever goes into your stomach is bound to affect your body's health, size, and shape. After all, we are often told "you are what you eat." These days, however, it seems few people are really happy with their own bodies.

Although you might find this difficult to believe, fat is essential for a healthy body. It stores energy, keeps you warm, and does many other important jobs. However, when it comes to eating fat, there are healthy kinds (*unsaturated fats*, as in some seeds and fish) and less-healthy kinds (*saturated fats*, as in butter, cheese, and cookies).

19 Many of your vital organs, especially the kidneys, heart, and intestines, are protected by fat. It helps to hold them in place and shields them from injury. Eating foods containing **fatty acids** is good for your organs.

Are you one of those people who would like to change the way you look?

20 Your body's fat affects your size, shape, and weight. Your genes influence the distribution of fat, but your eating and lifestyle do make a difference. A normal person has between 25 to 35 billion fat cells. The number can increase during times of weight gain, to as many as 100 to 150 billion cells.

21 Fat cells die at the rate of 150 per second. However, once a fat cell dies, the body makes a brand new one to take its place.

The right balance

Are you unhappy about your body shape? Then you are just like many other young people and adults! However, more people today than ever before do have too much body fat. This can be very harmful. Doctors use the term **obese** to describe someone at risk of developing health problems from being too heavy. While obesity affects some teens, others are so eager to look lean that they do not eat enough, which is just as unhealthy.

Teenagers in particular often feel pressure to change their body shape and size. However, between the ages of 12 and 18 the body is growing and changing more than ever, so it needs a balanced diet and exercise. Treat it right and learn to love your amazing body!

Think it through...

Are we too worried about how we look? Does seeing very thin people in movies, magazines, and on catwalks put too much pressure on us to look a certain way?

Gulp and Gasp

Food, water, and sleep are essential for your body to live, but you can manage without them for a while. That is not the case with your body's other requirement: oxygen. Without breathing in the oxygen in air, you would die in minutes.

What's the point in breathing?

You suck air into your lungs about 20 times per minute. First, that air is filtered, warmed, and moistened in your nose, before it goes down your windpipe into your lungs. Inside each of your lungs there are masses of tiny tubes called bronchioli. At the end of the bronchioli are millions of tiny sacs called alveoli. Inside the alveoli, the oxygen you have breathed in is absorbed into your bloodstream through tiny blood vessels called capillaries. There it is exchanged for waste carbon dioxide, which your body cells have made and which you will then breathe out.

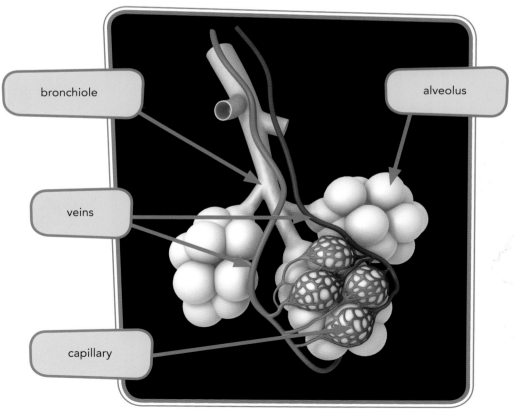

bronchiole

alveolus

veins

capillary

Breathtaking facts

22 Your lungs contain about 2,400 kilometers (1,500 miles) of airways and over 300 million alveoli. Spread out flat, all the alveoli would cover an area almost the size of half a tennis court.

23 When resting, you breathe in around 6 liters of air per minute. On average, you breathe in about 23,000 times a day. It's a good thing you do not have to think about every breath.

24 We tend to get more colds in the winter because we are indoors more often and much closer to other people. When people sneeze, cough, and breathe over you, germs go flying around. A sneeze blows out carbon dioxide, mucus, and germs from your mouth and nose at 160 kilometers per hour (100 miles per hour).

Manjit Singh has tried to break world records. Here, using just clamps and ropes, he is pulling a double-decker bus with his ears!

true story

Lung power

An average pair of adult human lungs can hold about 6 liters of air. However, only a small amount of this is used in normal breathing. A good fitness test is to measure your lung power—but you are not likely to beat "strongman" Manjit Singh. In 1998 Manjit broke a world record by blowing up a large weather balloon to a diameter of almost 2.5 meters (8 feet) in just 42 minutes. In 2009 Manjit appeared on a British television show. He puffed into a hot water bottle so hard that it blew up like a balloon and burst!

Hearty news

As soon as oxygen fills your lungs and enriches your blood, it has to get around your body to all the cells. That is thanks to your amazing heart—your body's pumping engine.

25 The average adult's body contains about 4.7 liters (5 quarts) of blood, which makes up about 7 percent of total body weight. Life-sustaining blood is constantly being pumped through your 97,000-kilometer- (60,000-mile-) long network of blood vessels. That is farther than twice around the world!

26 Your heart beats approximately 100,000 times a day, keeping your whole body supplied with oxygen and nutrients, while clearing away harmful wastes. That is about 30 million heartbeats a year!

27 A heartbeat is really the sound of the valves in the heart closing as they push blood through its chambers. An adult's heart pumps around 7,200 liters (1,900 gallons) of blood each day. By the age of 70, your heart will have pumped around 182 million liters (48 million gallons) of blood!

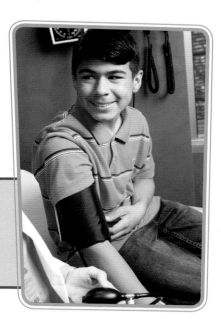

By measuring your blood pressure, a doctor can tell how effectively your blood is pumping through your body.

In 2007 the American Heart Association did a study into how high-energy drinks affect the heart. Within four hours of drinking one high-energy drink, the heart rate of the average adult went up by 8 percent. Although that is not dangerous to a healthy person, someone with heart disease could be at risk from too many cans of these drinks.

listen up!

Too much energy

In 2009, 17-year-old Jonathon VanGelderen, from Michigan, nearly died when his heart, which had a defect, started racing at over 200 beats per minute. The average heart rate is about 80 beats per minute. Too many high-energy drinks sent Jonathon's rapid heart rate into **cardiac arrest**, and he was rushed to the hospital. "I sort of felt like I had the flu," said Jonathon. But it was much worse than that, and doctors had to act fast to save him. They treated his damaged heart and said the **caffeine** in all his energy drinks had made it worse. After leaving the hospital, Jonathan said, "I don't have caffeine or anything like that anymore and I try to watch what I eat." Now he can look forward to enjoying life with a healthier heart.

28 The human heart creates enough pressure to squirt blood for a distance of 9 meters (29.5 feet). If you give a tennis ball a hard squeeze, you are using about the same amount of force your heart uses to pump blood out to the body. Even when you are resting, your heart's muscles are still hard at work, keeping your blood flowing.

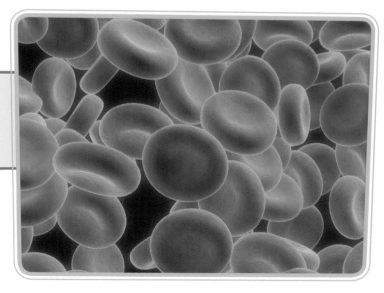

These are red blood cells seen under a microscope.

29 The millions of blood cells racing round your veins bring nourishment, **hormones**, vitamins, and antibodies to your body. Made in your **bone marrow**, the red blood cells carry oxygen and carbon dioxide, while your white blood cells fight infections and disease.

Things you'd like to know but can't always ask:

Why doesn't my belly button heal up?

30 The belly button (navel) is scar tissue from where your **umbilical cord** was cut just after you were born. It does not heal up because there is nothing between it and your stomach except a few thin layers of skin.

What's that?

The **umbilical cord** passes nourishment to a fetus by connecting it to its mother.

Does your hair keep growing after you die?

31 It was once thought that fingernails and hair continued to grow after a person died. In fact, nothing on the body really grows after death. The hair and nails just appear to get longer as the skin shrivels and draws back.

Are we shorter at night than we are in the morning?

32 All of us are tallest in the morning, shorter in the afternoon, and shortest at night. Adults "shrink" during the day, as the spine compresses by an average of 15 millimeters (0.6 inches). Resting at night loosens the spine again.

Why do I blush when I feel embarrassed?

33 When you are embarrassed or upset, your body releases a hormone called **adrenaline**. This speeds up your breathing and heart rate, which increases the blood flow to parts of your body, including your face. A surge of blood reaches your cheeks and you turn red.

Why do you get a black eye after a blow to the face?

34 The skin around your eyes is loose, with mostly fat underneath. Fluid collects there easily. After a blow to your face or the head, blood and fluids collect in the space around your eyes. The skin darkens and "puffs up." Most black eyes are minor injuries and will heal after a few days.

Even wizards get black eyes!

Daniel Radcliffe, the actor who plays Harry Potter, got a black
eye while filming a fight scene for *Harry Potter and the Deathly
Hallows*. He said, "I was shooting a scene where Harry is fighting
a huge snake. Instead of an actual snake in front of me, our stunt
coordinator held a long stick with a boxing glove at the end. He got
me by surprise and hit me in the face. The blow was strong enough
to knock me out! I saw the scene on slow motion afterward, and it
looks like I get hit like a real boxer. Really classy!"

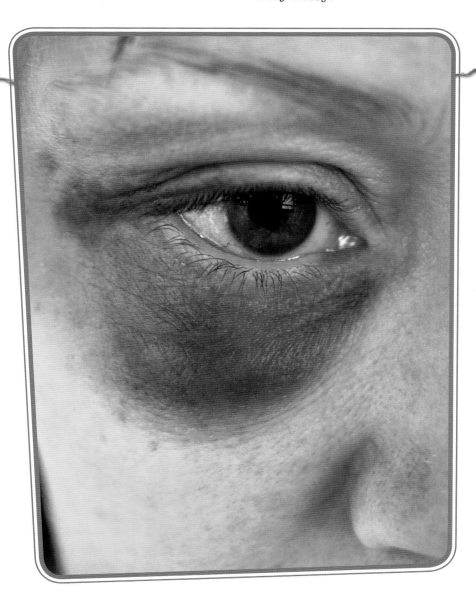

How Embarrassing

Despite being amazing, your body can sometimes let you down in front of others. It can unexpectedly leak, smell, makes noises, or suddenly look weird.

Smelly things

When you reach your teens, your body can start to do strange things that can take you by surprise. One of them is sweating like never before. That is because the millions of sweat glands in a teenager's skin "switch on." This can make your skin extra damp and smelly. So the big question is: Why?

35
You have two sorts of sweat glands:

- Apocrine glands, like those in your armpits, are really scent glands. The sweat that comes from them has a particular smell. It can even attract people! You have about one million of these glands on your body.

- Eccrine glands make you sweat when you are hot. You have about three million of these glands all over your body. Every square centimeter of your back has about 60 sweat glands. On the palms of your hands and soles of your feet you have about 600 glands per square centimeter.

36
Sweat on your skin and clothes soon becomes a breeding ground for bacteria. The bacteria break down the sweat to make fatty acids. These give off an unpleasant stale-sweat smell. Arm and groin sweat is rich in protein, which attracts bacteria. That is why regular washing, fresh clothes, and **deodorants** are a good idea to stop smelly body odor.

1 cm

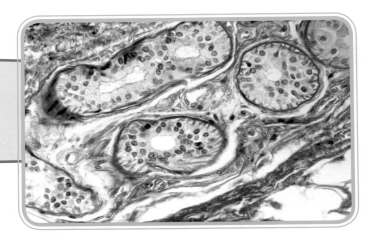

The skin has many sweat glands that can be seen under a microscope.

Sweat helps to keep your body cool.

Temperature control

37 When you get hot, your brain signals to your body to start cooling itself down. Your sweat glands "switch on," and blood flows closer to your body's surface and away from your heart. Sweat **evaporates** from your body to help cool you down.

38 Sweat glands are all over the body, except on your nails, ears, and lips. It may feel like you sweat most under your arms. That is because air cannot get under your arms very easily, so sweat evaporates there less quickly than other parts of your body. In fact, you sweat more under your arms when you are standing up than if you are sitting or lying down.

39 Every day your sweat glands excrete an average of nearly 1 liter (1.1 quarts) of moisture. If you take part in sports, go for a long run, or are out on a very hot day, you could sweat as much as 10 liters (10.5 quarts) in a day.

Females have more sweat glands than males. However, a male's sweat glands are more active, which is why men tend to sweat more than women.

listen up!

Yucky things

One of the biggest embarrassments to hit young people is a face that erupts into a mass of oozing pimples. Although **acne** can affect anyone at any age, it strikes about 80 percent of teenagers.

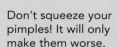
Don't squeeze your pimples! It will only make them worse.

Your skin has oil in it called sebum. Many teens make too much sebum when their hormones become active. This means that the pores in their skin clog up. The pores get infected, red, and swollen, which causes nasty pimples. There are all kinds of myths about acne:

Myth 1: Chocolate and greasy foods cause acne

40 Although eating too much fatty food is not a good idea, studies show that no particular food causes acne. Some people notice their pimples are worse after eating certain foods, but a few French fries won't cause them.

Myth 2: Popping pimples will get rid of them

41 By squeezing pimples, you can push bacteria into the skin and make them far worse. Sometimes the marks left by popped pimples can last many months. Some scars leave dents or pits forever. The pus inside pimples is a thick white or yellowish fluid that forms in areas of infection. It is a mix of **decomposed** body tissue, bacteria, and white blood cells.

Myth 3: Pimples disappear if you scrub your face

42 Although washing the face gets rid of dirt and oil from your pores, washing too much can rub the skin and cause more pimples. It is best to wash your face about twice a day with mild soap and water. Then gently pat it dry. If the acne gets worse, there are many treatments available that help to clear the skin.

43 Warts are round, thick lumps of skin, like little grayish cauliflowers. They are caused by a virus. Some people get just one or two. Others can get lots, and they keep coming back. Warts are not harmful, and there are treatments that can get rid of them. However, warts are infectious, or spread from person to person.

44 If you get warts on your hands: DO keep your hands clean, but don't wash them too often. Washing your hands won't get rid of warts. It is best to see a doctor or pharmacist to get the right treatment. DON'T pick or scratch warts. Scratching might spread the virus to another part of your body. If you have a wart on your hand, you should not touch anyone else with that hand. But there is no truth in the myth that you can catch warts from toads!

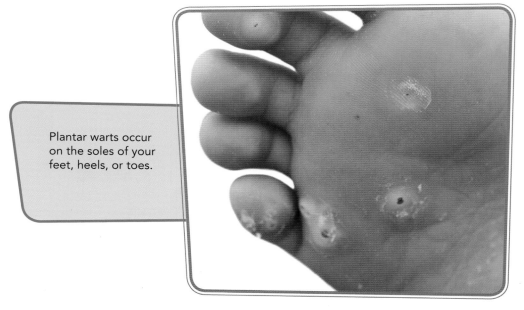

Plantar warts occur on the soles of your feet, heels, or toes.

45 A plantar wart is a wart on the sole of the foot. It is the same as a common wart, but the weight of the body presses it into the foot, which can be painful.

Hairy things

What can be more embarrassing than hair growing in places or ways you do not want it to grow? Just take a look at all the hair products around to see how much we spend trying to change our hair—or to remove it.

Hair is made up of dead protein called **keratin**. It is the same material that makes up fingernails, toenails, and teeth in humans and horns and hooves in animals.

46 Believe it or not, hair covers your whole body, apart from the soles of your feet, the palms of your hands, and your lips. The shape of your hair **follicles** determines whether your hair is curly, wavy, or straight. A follicle is the small cavity from which a hair grows. If a follicle is flat, it produces curly hair. Round hair follicles produce straight hair.

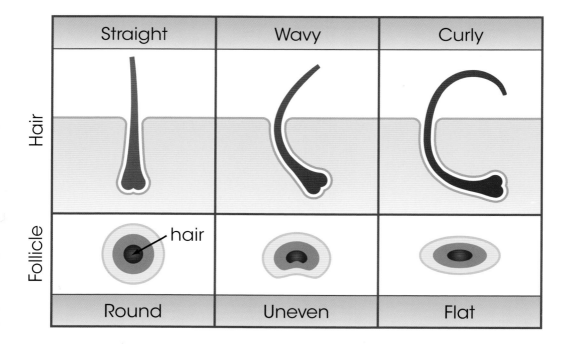

Straight	Wavy	Curly
Round	Uneven	Flat

Hair

Follicle

hair

47 You cannot always see them, but you have five million hairs on your body! This is as many as a chimpanzee has. Most of your hairs are too fine and light to be noticed.

48 The life span of each human hair is from three to seven years. About 80 hairs are likely to fall out of your head every day. But you do not need to worry, as you probably have about 100,000 hair follicles. Lost hairs are normally replaced when a new hair grows back in the same follicle. Hair loss in adults usually occurs when the hair follicles start to shrink. This makes hair thinner and weaker, and it causes what is called "pattern baldness."

49 A rare condition called hypertrichosis causes extra growth of hair in areas where hair does not normally grow. It may grow thickly over the entire body, or it could be in just a few areas. Some people are born with the condition, and others develop it later on in life. It is sometimes called "werewolf syndrome."

Despite what many people believe, shaving does not change the texture, color, or rate of new hair growth. It just looks and feels coarser because it has flat, recently cut ends.

listen up!

Some hairy facts

- The longest human hair in the world measures over 5 meters (16.4 feet)!

- If the average male never shaved, his beard would be 4 meters (13.1 feet) long in his seventies!

- Blonde people tend to have more hairs on their bodies than dark-haired people do.

Noisy things

How embarrassing. You go to a friend's house and in front of the whole family, you sit down and your body rumbles. Gas escapes with a loud noise and a nasty smell. Oops! It may not help your embarrassment, but everybody on the planet passes gas every day. It is actually a sign of a healthy body. But it is best not to do it too often in public.

Passing gas can be both a noisy thing *and* a smelly thing!

50 The average human releases 0.5 to 2.5 liters (0.5 to 2.6 quarts) of gas per day. That is enough to fill a balloon. You are not always aware of the releasing gas unless it smells or makes a noise. Most people are estimated to pass gas on average 12 times per day.

51 Body gas results from the bacteria in your large intestine breaking down eaten food and causing it to ferment. This produces gases such as nitrogen, carbon dioxide, hydrogen, and methane. Most of these gases are absorbed back into the body, but the rest escapes— sometimes when you least expect it.

52 Depending on what you eat, and the type of bacteria in your large intestine, you might produce the gas hydrogen sulfide. When that gas escapes, everyone will know about it because it smells a little like rotten eggs.

53 Foods that are high in fiber, such as bran, beans, fruit, garlic, cabbage, and cauliflower, tend to make a lot of gas inside you. Although these high-fiber foods can give you gas, they are also good for you. Eating food too fast and gulping in air when chewing will also increase your body gases. The buildup of gases and their release is called flatulence.

54 Burps or belches are the sound of gas leaving your body from your stomach and out through your mouth. In addition to the air that enters your stomach when you eat, drinking carbonated drinks will also add to the gas in your stomach. All those bubbles are carbon dioxide. When they escape, they can rush up with an embarrassing noise, often before you can cover your mouth politely.

Le Pétomane was the stage name of a French entertainer named Joseph Pujol (1857–1945). His stage name came from the French word *peter*, "to fart." Pujol was famous for having remarkable control of his abdominal muscles. He could pass gas to music and play tunes from his behind!

listen up!

Cow power

Cows burp a lot! Scientists have calculated that every year cows in the United States burp about 45 million tonnes (50 million tons) of gases into the atmosphere. The gas from the burps of 10 cows could keep a small house heated for a year.

Problem page

Sometimes your embarrassing body can take you by surprise . . .

Problem: You meet that perfect person and you are eager to make the right impression. But then it all goes horribly wrong. Just as you get close, they hold their nose and back away. Looks like you have a problem you didn't know you had—bad breath. How did that happen?

55 One cause of bad breath is bacteria in the mouth. If you do not brush and floss regularly, bacteria grow on the bits of food left in your mouth and between your teeth. Some foods, such as garlic and onions, can make matters worse. Mouthwash and mints only cover your smelly breath for a while, and mints containing sugar can damage your teeth. Clean your teeth for at least two minutes, at least twice a day, to remove any extra bacteria.

Problem: You come back from a great vacation in the sun, but instead of a super-cool tan, your face is covered in freckles. Why is that?

56 When you go out in the sun, the ultraviolet (UV) rays in sunshine make your cells produce more **melanin**. This makes your freckles darker. Freckles soon fade, but freckly or not, you should always use sunblock to protect your skin when you go out in the sun.

Problem: It is a night you've been waiting for, that special occasion when you want to look your best. But your shoulders look like you have been in a snowstorm. Dandruff is a common problem, but is it serious?

57 Dandruff is flakes of skin from the scalp. It can affect people for all kinds of reasons, such as stress, diet, weather, or hormones. A flaking scalp is not infectious. Nor has it anything to do with bad hygiene or dirty hair. You can help control dandruff by washing your hair regularly with a medicated shampoo. Until the dandruff stops, it is best not to wear dark tops that will make it show up even more.

Freckles are perfectly normal. They will become darker when you have been out in the sun, but will soon fade again.

What's that?

Melanin is a substance found in the skin, hair, and eyes. It makes your skin darker when you are exposed to sunlight.

Baffling Brains

If you thought your heart, stomach, and other body parts were amazing, just wait until you read about your brain. Humans have the most complex and remarkable brains of any creatures on Earth.

Your brain never stops regulating your body. It controls your breathing and heart rate without you even noticing. It coordinates your movements, and it is the center of all your ideas, feelings, thoughts, creativity, and consciousness.

58 A newborn baby's brain almost triples in size during its first year. Most areas of your brain stop growing when you are about 15 years old.

59 Your brain has more than 100 billion **neurons**. The brain sends electric pulses that act as commands to other parts of your body through neurons. These pulses create enough electricity to power a lightbulb. In fact, your brain uses more energy than any other organ, burning up 20 percent of the food you eat.

60 The right side of your brain controls muscles on the left side of your body, and the left side of your brain controls muscles on the right side of your body. Messages from the left side of your body cross over to the right side of your brain, and vice versa. This means that damage to one side of the brain will affect the opposite side of the body.

61 Your brain is busy processing thousands of thoughts every hour. Information travels at different speeds within different types of neurons. Transmission can be as slow as 0.5 meters (1.6 feet) per second, or as fast as 120 meters (394 feet) per second. This is about 435 kilometers (270 miles) per hour.

62 Your brain needs a constant supply of oxygen. If one of the oxygen-delivering vessels breaks, or becomes blocked, the brain begins to starve. This would cause you to have a **stroke**. Your brain can live for four to six minutes without oxygen before it begins to die. With no oxygen for five to ten minutes, the brain will be permanently damaged.

Brain power

Phineas Gage experienced one of the most amazing cases of survival after brain damage. He was also the first patient from whom scientists learned about the function of the front of the brain and its relationship to personality.

In 1848, at age 25, Phineas was a railroad worker in Vermont. He was packing explosives, when they suddenly went off. A long iron rod flew up and hit him in the left cheek. The rod went straight through his skull and came out of the top of his brain. Phineas did not lose consciousness, but he became confused. He lived for 12 more years, which amazed all his doctors. His injury made him lose sight in one eye. It also changed his personality, making him aggressive. This was the result of damage to the "mood control" area at the front of his brain.

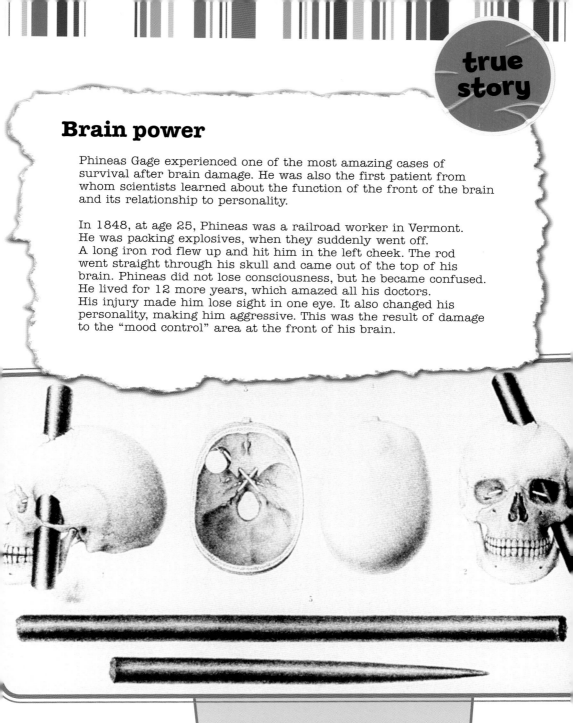

Phineas Gage's skull and the iron rod are in a museum in Boston.

Good sense

The brain is the nerve center that makes sense of a constant stream of messages and sensations. In addition to sight, hearing, smell, taste, and touch, humans have other sensations that the brain interprets such as balance, pressure, temperature, pain, and motion. You are continually making sense of the world around you through your sensory organs. These can transmit millions of messages to your brain in a second.

63 *Sight*: When an image is formed on the back of your eye, it is upside-down. Your brain makes you see it the right way up. Your brain also merges the two images captured by each of your eyes into one. By doing this, your brain creates a three-dimensional picture.

64 *Hearing*: Your ears do not just allow you to hear. They also give you your sense of balance. Your ear has over 25,000 tiny hair cells to help you hear sounds. At birth, the human ear can hear sounds lower than the lowest note on a piano and sounds higher than the highest note on a piccolo. A major reason for hearing loss is exposure to very loud noises. Being just in front of the speakers at a concert can damage your hearing after only a few minutes.

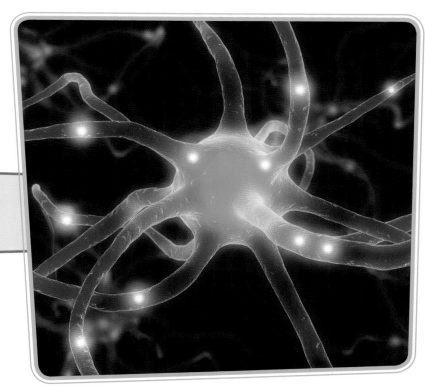

This is an image of a neuron.

65 *Smell*: If your nose is working well, you should be able to tell the difference between 4,000 to 10,000 smells. There are about 10 million smell receptors in the space behind your nose, but they get weaker as you grow older. Your sense of smell is around 10,000 times more sensitive than your sense of taste.

66 *Taste*: There are up to 8,000 taste buds on your tongue (children have more than adults). Taste buds detect sweet, sour, salty, savory (known as *umami*), and bitter flavors. Tasting is about 80 percent smell, and your sense of smell increases when you are hungry. Over a 12-day period, your body makes a whole new set of taste buds.

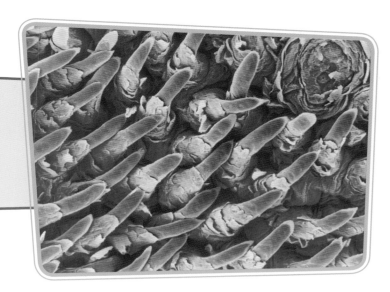

Smoking, alcohol, caffeine, spicy and hot foods, onions, and garlic dull your taste buds, shown here.

67 *Touch*: You have at least five different types of nerve endings all over your skin. Most of these touch receptors are for pain. Others are sensitive to temperature, pressure, or irritation. Your skin is least sensitive in the middle of your back. It is most sensitive in your hands, fingertips, and lips.

Memories

Scents often remind us of events from a long time ago. When we first smell a new scent, we link it to an event, a person, an object, or a place. Our brains then make a link between that smell and a memory. Because we first smell new scents when we are young, certain smells often remind us of our childhood.

Quiz

1. Why do your ears make wax?
   a. to help protect them from loud noises
   b. to keep out germs and creepy crawlies
   c. to get rid of waste brain cells
   d. it has no use at all

2. What is the colored part of your eye called?
   a. pupil
   b. retina
   c. iris
   d. lens

3. How long can your body survive without food and water?
   a. without food for a week and without water for three days
   b. without food for about a month and about a week without water
   c. without food and water for about ten days
   d. without food and water for almost six months if you lie down

4. Which part of you can you live without?
   a. your head
   b. your heart
   c. your lungs
   d. your appendix

34

Fast facts about your appendix:

68 Your appendix is attached to the first part of your large intestine. It is a small tube about the same size as your little finger.

69 In some animals, the appendix helps with digestion. However, in humans it no longer plays this role. It is thought that when early humans discovered how to cook their food, the appendix was no longer needed. It became smaller and smaller over time.

70 Doctors continue to argue about whether the human appendix has any use at all. In an adult, the appendix has no real purpose. However, during a baby's first few years of life it is part of the immune system.

71 Sometimes the appendix can become infected and cause appendicitis. This can be painful and also harmful if the appendix "bursts." Leaving an infected appendix untreated can be dangerous, so it needs to be removed by surgery. This is a safe and simple operation.

true story

A famous appendix

In 2008 Zac Efron, the star of *High School Musical*, was rushed to the hospital to have his infected appendix removed. The actor, who starred as Troy Bolton in the hit movie, had the operation at a Los Angeles hospital and made a speedy recovery. Phew!

Sweet Dreams

Regular sleep is essential for your body and brain. You spend one-third of your life sleeping. This can be well over 25 years in bed in an average lifetime! The length and quality of your sleep affects your daily behavior, your mood, and your entire waking life. You can even die from lack of sleep. Scientists are still discovering many of sleep's secrets. Sleep helps to keep you healthy by slowing your body's systems down to reenergize you after each day's activities. So, are you getting enough sleep?

72 These are some of the signs that you may need more sleep each night:
- difficulty waking up in the morning
- unable to concentrate
- falling asleep during the day
- feeling moody and depressed.

73 There is a lot going on in your body even when you are asleep. For example, you may change positions as many as 40 times during a night. Your brain does not shut down, either. Studies show that brain waves are just as active while you are sleeping as when you are awake.

74 Most people dream for about one or two hours per night and have an average of four to seven dreams. If you wake up during a dream, you are much more likely to remember the dream than if you sleep soundly for a full night's sleep.

Teenagers need an average of 9.2 hours of sleep each night, or about an hour more than older and younger age groups. Very small children, the biggest sleepers, need up to 18 hours of sleep each day.

listen up!

Sleep stages

1. *Light sleep*: You are half asleep and your muscles relax, with some slight twitching.
2. *True sleep*: Your breathing and heart rate slow down.
3. *Deep sleep*: Your brain waves are busy, but your breathing and heart rate fall further.
4. *REM* (*Rapid Eye Movement*) *sleep*: This usually begins about 70 to 90 minutes after you fall asleep. Your eyes dart around as your breathing rate and blood pressure rise. This is when most dreams occur. You will have around three to five REM episodes a night.

Do not lean on door

Some people can fall asleep anywhere, especially if they go to bed too late!

true story

Don't try this at home

Randy Gardner, a 17-year-old Californian student, set the record for the longest period without sleep in 1964. He lasted 11 days (264 hours) without sleep. Four days into the research, he began hallucinating (seeing things). He then became confused and thought he was a famous football player. His efforts have reportedly been surpassed since, but Guinness World Records stopped recognizing records for sleeplessness due to the potential bad effects on health.

Strange, but True...

Sleep has always been full of mystery. Not only has the meaning of our dreams troubled us through the ages, but it is also a fact that some people do strange things in their sleep. Just what is going on in our bodies and minds when we "shut down"?

The unconscious brain can do puzzling things. Why would someone who is fast asleep suddenly sit up and go for a walk without waking up?

76 Sleepwalking affects all ages, but it happens most often in children ages 6 to 12. Sleepwalking seems to run in families. Some sleepwalkers pick things up, move things around, get dressed, leave the house, or even drive a car! Sleepwalking can last a few seconds to a few minutes, but it can sometimes last for over half an hour.

77 A "sleep center" in the brain controls sleeping and waking. When you sleep, the sleep center blocks off a part of the brain to stop nerves from sending out signals. Your body remains still. But sometimes the mechanism can fail. When this happens, messages get through to the body even though the brain is sleeping. The body "stays awake" and walks. Sleepwalkers usually have no memory of what they did.

78 Boys are more likely to sleepwalk than girls. About 18 percent of people worldwide are affected by sleepwalking at various times. Sleepwalking only occurs during deep sleep.

Sleep paralysis

Some people can be fast asleep on their backs when they suddenly wake but cannot move or speak. This is called sleep paralysis. It can last for seconds to several minutes, causing fear and panic. It happens because of a "disconnection" between the brain and the body. Sleep paralysis is thought to affect about half of us some time in our lives.

Sleep disorder

REM-Sleep Behavior Disorder (RBD) is when some people act out their dreams when asleep. If their dream is very active, the sleeper can become violent and swear, shout, kick, and even fight. These people must wake up exhausted!

Sleepwalker rescued from top of giant crane

In 2005 a young sleepwalker was rescued after being found fast asleep over 40 meters (131 feet) up the arm of a construction crane. Emergency services were called to a building site in London, England, after a passerby spotted the 15-year-old girl curled up high above the ground. She had climbed up the crane and walked across a narrow metal beam while fast asleep. The girl had sleepwalked from her home and headed straight for the crane. The rescue took two hours, and the girl was finally carried off the crane and brought down. At around 4:00 a.m. she was taken to the hospital for a checkup, before being sent home. Luckily, she was unharmed.

The technical name for sleepwalking is *somnambulism*.

Growing Up

When you are growing up, the changes that are happening in your body can feel pretty scary if you are not prepared for them. During the teenage years, as **puberty** sets in, all kinds of changes are underway. These are all perfectly normal, but they can sometimes take you by surprise.

Some boys have a hard time when their voice starts cracking, squeaking, and generally sounding weird. What's going on? These signs simply mean that your voice is "breaking." The voice box (larynx) is zapped by a hormone called testosterone. This is released into the body from the **testicles**. Testosterone affects the vocal cords, making them longer and thicker. This makes the boy's voice sound lower. Some boys' voices break smoothly, but others have a rougher ride.

An Adam's apple looks like a small, round apple just under the skin in the front of the throat.

79 Boys' vocal cords stretch over the windpipe like small, thin elastic bands. As the vocal cords grow, they push out in a little bump in the throat, known as the Adam's apple. While the Adam's apple and vocal cords are growing, one minute you can sound like Mickey Mouse and the next you are grunting like Darth Vader! But look on the bright side. Some scientists think the male voice deepens to attract girls and scare off other male competition. So, a wobbly voice is healthy and normal for teenage boys.

Help! What are periods?

All girls going through puberty take time to get used to their monthly periods. These bodily changes can start any time between the ages of 8 and 13. This is when hormones begin to affect the body like never before.

A period, known as **menstruation**, happens once a month, although times can vary. This is when a girl's **uterus** sheds an unfertilized egg, with a small amount of blood (about four to six tablespoons).

What's that?

A **uterus** is a muscular organ in a woman's body where a fetus grows. The uterus is also called the womb.

80 Three facts about menstruation:
- The normal time each period (menstrual cycle) lasts is 28 to 35 days.
- On average, a period lasts two to seven days.
- The average amount of blood lost is 35 milliliters (1.2 fluid ounces).

Many girls have stomach cramps during the first few days of their periods. These cramps are usually caused by chemicals produced by the body that make the muscles of the uterus contract. Some girls also get headaches. But the good news is you feel fine again in a few days, and periods show your changing body is healthy and normal.

What's Going on Down There?

As you grow up, your sexual organs are developing to enable **reproduction** when you become an adult. Here are some common questions and answers about what is going on "down there."

Girls

Why am I changing shape down there? Why are my hips and waist changing shape?

Your body shape has to change to help you to cope with childbirth when the time comes.

Boys

Why do my testicles give me pain?

Testicles can be sensitive to pain because of the mass of nerve endings inside them. Testicles produce sperm, so the body makes them sensitive to make sure a male carefully protects them. Nerves from the testicles are connected to the abdomen, so pain is often felt in the stomach after a hit to the groin.

81 One cause of pain in growing boys is a "twisted testicle." This condition needs to be treated by a doctor. The testicle suddenly becomes very painful and swells because the nerves and blood vessels become twisted. The twisted testicle needs to be quickly and carefully untangled with surgery.

82 Everyone develops according to his or her own biological clock. Some boys can start developing as early as 10 years old. Others can start much later. As you get taller and bulkier, your shoulders broaden and your muscles get stronger. Your penis and testicles also enlarge—but all this takes time.

83 During puberty, boys can experience growth spurts almost overnight. This can cause all kinds of adjustment problems, including trouble with coordination skills. It often makes for a clumsy or awkward time, as hands and feet suddenly grow much larger.

Bodily changes during puberty can cause a lot of anxiety.

84 During puberty, a girl's body shape becomes curvier. At this time it is normal to gain weight, especially around the hips and stomach, so going on a crash diet is not a good idea.

A lot is growing at this time. Bones grow bigger and stronger to make the frame sturdier, internal organs grow larger, and the shape of the body changes as muscles become stronger and firmer. Hormonal changes will affect body odor, with increased perspiration, especially under the arms. Hair will grow under the arms, too, as well as around the vagina. Hairs on the legs and upper lip may also grow more.

85 The average adolescent girl has between 300,000 and 400,000 egg follicles. However, only about 350 eggs (one per month) will mature during her lifetime. Monthly menstrual cycles cease when a woman reaches her forties or fifties.

86 Sperm is made in a male's testicles. It takes about 72 days for one sperm to grow. Approximately 85 million sperm are produced each day by each testicle. Sperm continue to be produced throughout a man's life. That could be over 1,000,000,000,000 sperm in his lifetime!

Moods and Stress

Another likely result of all those hormones going around a teenager's body is "attitude." Some young people feel like they are on a roller coaster of moods. One minute they are giggling, and the next they are feeling sad, confused, or angry.

All these mood swings can be confusing, stressful, and upsetting. Your body and brain are adjusting to all the "strange" chemicals racing through your veins. But by the end of puberty, your hormone levels readjust. You will start to feel like the roller coaster is back on a calmer track.

87 The hormones produced during puberty reshape an adolescent's brain structure. This is the cause of all those mood swings and stress. These issues continue until the brain finishes maturing.

88 Feeling stressed out is very common during puberty. Studies show that the largest stress-causing issues for young people are school, parents, and friends. Teenage girls are affected by stress more than boys, but girls are usually better at asking for help from others during a stressful time. Talking to others about feelings can be very useful.

89 Researchers have found that the age when puberty begins has been falling for the past 150 years. It has dropped three years within the past century alone, as a result of better public health and improved nutrition. But stress is another reason. Children feeling great stress in their lives tend to reach puberty earlier than average.

90 Too much stress is unhealthy for the body and mind. Some of the symptoms are stomachaches, headaches, feeling exhausted, loss of appetite, poor concentration, and trouble sleeping. These can have a negative effect on schoolwork, family life, and friendships.

Quiz

Take the stress test to see if you know the causes and effects of stress and ways to deal with it.

1. Whom do you talk to when you are stressed out?
    a. no one—I don't need to
    b. anybody I can find
    c. a good friend

2. What do you do when you feel stressed out?
    a. eat a huge plate of French fries
    b. go for a run and get a good night's sleep
    c. cry and watch three DVDs

3. What are your usual signs of being stressed out?
    a. upset stomach and headaches
    b. getting colds and feeling run-down
    c. tense muscles and loss of sleep
    d. all of the above
    e. none of these

Find out the truth!

1. c. Talk to someone you know well.
2. b. Exercise and rest are great stress-busters.
3. d. A bad dose of stress can give you all these symptoms and more.

Do some people make you mad? Blame those hormones!

45

Extreme Bodies

Your body isn't just amazing. It also has some extraordinary design features. Your skeleton has to cope with all the wear and tear of daily life. It is a wonder of engineering that enables you to do many things.

Great joints

Your joints are the hinges that connect bones together. They allow you to move easily. Ball-and-socket joints (such as your hips and shoulders) have rounded ends on bones that fit into bone hollows, allowing movement in all directions.

91 When you run, the impact on your legs is three times your body weight. When you jump, the impact on your skeleton can reach 10 times your body weight. Your knee is a very complex joint with cartilage, which is made of a tough elastic material called collagen (a protein "glue" that helps hold the body together). This absorbs a lot of the shocks to your knees.

92 Your knee joints are held together by fibers called tendons and ligaments, which stretch as the joint bends, but act like really tough threads of nylon rope. The human skeleton is built from super-strong bones that are tougher than concrete. Even so, joints and bones can fail and cause a lot of pain.

93 Osteoporosis is a disease that weakens the bones, and it affects millions of people. One in two women and one in five men over the age of 50 will have a fracture because of it. Eating calcium-rich foods and exercising can help maintain good bone density. Weight-bearing exercise like soccer helps to strengthen and maintain healthy bones.

Being "double-jointed" means that your joints and surrounding tissue are unusually flexible, enabling you to bend or rotate them in ways that other people find impossible.

Muscles

Much of your power and strength comes from your muscles, so it pays to take good care of them. You do not have to pump iron to be fit and strong. Just being active keeps your muscles flexible, gives your heart and lungs a good workout, and gets the blood going to the brain. What do you know about muscles?

94 Every time you move a muscle, it contracts (shrinks and tightens). Exercise makes muscles contract hard, over and over again. This increases the blood supply to the muscle being worked and makes it bigger, stronger, and able to work longer without getting tired.

95 The largest muscle in your body is what you sit on. Its proper name is the gluteus maximus muscle in the buttocks. But your strongest muscle relative to its size is your tongue. You probably exercise that one a lot! In fact, you also use about another 70 muscles for speaking.

96 You have over 30 muscles in your face, which you use to show surprise, happiness, or sadness. Try looking in the mirror and watch them at work. The tiny muscles in your eyes are the busiest of all. Scientists think they may move more than 100,000 times a day.

Beyond Belief

In extreme situations, the human body can sometimes do incredible things. Unexpected reserves of energy and endurance can have surprising results.

Adrenaline is a hormone that your body releases when you need super powers. It is sometimes called the "fight or flight" hormone because it gives a surge of energy if you need to attack or run when under threat. Adrenaline quickens your heartbeat and opens up the airways of your lungs, so you are ready for action.

97 Adrenaline helps the body's fuel (glucose) to get instant energy to muscles. Some scientists think we use only a small amount of our muscles' power. The rush of adrenaline can supply a sudden burst of extra strength, and sometimes it makes us perform wonders!

Some people enjoy extreme sports just for the adrenaline rush!

Extreme endorphins

Your body has another trick for giving yourself a boost when you most need it. Special chemicals, called **endorphins**, are produced during exercise, pain, and excitement.

98 Endorphins, produced in the brain, are your natural anti-depressants. They can give a sense of well-being during stress, boost confidence, and calm you down.

99 In addition to exercise, some foods can boost the production of the brain's "feel-good" endorphins. Chocolate and chili peppers are known to have this effect.

100 Listening to music may be good for your heart. In 2008 researchers at the University of Maryland, in Baltimore, demonstrated that joyful music can have a healthy effect on your blood vessels. One of the researchers, Dr. Michael Miller, says, "Listening to music evokes positive emotions likely to release endorphins—part of that mind–heart connection that we want to learn more about."

101 A study of rowers at Oxford University, in England, in 2009 found that team members who exercised together could cope with twice as much discomfort and pain as when they trained on their own. Endorphin release seems to be far greater in groups than in individual training. This may also explain the positive feelings of belonging we have when we do group exercise and sports.

true story

Natural painkillers

In 2003 Amy Racina was hiking alone in California's Kings Canyon, when she fell nearly 20 meters (65 feet) onto solid rock. She broke her right foot, shin, and knee. Her left leg was smashed at the thigh. Amy's brain released endorphins as her natural painkillers. She had fallen in an area far away from any help and needed to get herself off the mountain. After crawling for two days, she was rescued and could finally relax. But—OUCH! The endorphins stopped working. She said: "The moment I truly felt the pain was when I was loaded into the stretcher. It was absolutely excruciating."

Top Ten Tips

Take good care of your body—it's the only one you have! Here are some tips to help you keep it in top condition:

1. Eat well
Your body needs energy to live and grow. There are three main sources of energy from food: carbohydrates, protein, and fat. You need a mix of all three to stay healthy.

2. Eat wisely
Fried food is fine now and then, but not too often. Too much fatty food (such as French fries cooked in saturated fat) can be bad for the heart. Choose lean meat, fish, poultry without skin, and low-fat dairy food whenever you can.

3. Eat fiber
Eat five or six portions of fruits and vegetables each day—as well as cereals, rice, pasta, brown bread, and bran—to keep your insides working!

4. Eat a balanced diet
Variety is the spice of life, and that applies to eating, too. A balanced diet has plenty of different vitamins, minerals, colors, and flavors. Eating a balanced diet provides sources of energy and nutrition for growth and development. The usual advice is to eat at least three balanced meals a day. And DON'T skip breakfast!

5. Exercise
Regular exercise is good for muscles and joints. Your lungs and heart will benefit, too. It does not have to be too active or tiring, but a brisk walk, bicycle ride, or game of tennis are examples of ideal kinds of exercise.

6. Drink plenty of water
Regular sips of water are good for you. Try to drink about eight glasses every day.

7. Sleep
Are you getting eight or nine hours of good sleep each night? Your body and brain need regular sleep at night if they are to keep you going for years on end.

8. You are what you eat
Remember to read food labels to spot the hidden sugar and chemicals in food. Fast food and pre-packaged meals often have hidden salt. Too much salt can be bad for you.

9. Hygiene
Wash, scrub, and shower to keep your skin and teeth clean from bacteria, smells, and infections.

10. Avoid bad decisions
Stay away from alcohol, tobacco, and drugs if you want to stay really fit and keep your body at its best.

Glossary

acne skin problem marked by pimples, especially on the face

adrenaline hormone that acts on the muscles of the body to give a short burst of energy

antibody substance produced by special cells in the body to fight infection

bacterium (plural: **bacteria**) simple, single-celled organisms that exist either alone or in colonies

bone marrow soft tissue rich in blood vessels that fills the cavities of most bones

caffeine substance found in some high-energy drinks, as well as coffee and tea

cardiac arrest occurs when the heart develops such an abnormal rhythm that it causes it to stop beating suddenly

cholesterol waxy substance in the blood that can clog arteries if found in large amounts

decompose to break down, or rot, and undergo a chemical change

deodorant chemical that destroys or masks unpleasant body smells

endorphin chemical produced by the brain that has a "feel good" effect

epidemic disease that affects many people at once

evaporate turn from liquid into vapor (a gas)

excrete get rid of waste, such as sweat, urine, or feces, from the body

fatty acid basic building block of fats. Your body needs fatty acids to work properly.

feces waste from the body discharged through the anus

follicle small hole in the skin from which a hair grows

hormone chemical that affects how cells function

immune having resistance to an illness or disease

keratin protein that makes up hair and hard tissues such as fingernails

melanin substance found in the skin, hair, and eyes. Melanin makes skin darker when it is exposed to sunlight.

menstruation monthly discharge of blood and tissue waste from a female's uterus

mucus sticky substance produced in the body to moisten and protect

mutate go through genetic changes

neuron cell that transmits messages from the brain

obese being more than 20 percent over the ideal weight for your height

parasite living thing that lives in or on another living thing

plaque sticky film on teeth that is formed by and contains bacteria

puberty age when children begin producing sex hormones and grow into adults

reproduction sexual process of creating a baby

stroke sudden loss of consciousness or the power to move, caused by a damaged blood vessel in the brain

testicles two oval-shaped glands that produce sperm and testosterone

toxin chemical containing some form of poison

ulcer open sore in which tissue breaks down and sometimes heals very slowly

umbilical cord cord-like structure that passes nourishment to a fetus by connecting it to its mother

uterus muscular organ in a woman's body, where a fetus grows. The uterus is also called the womb.

Find Out More

Books

Ditkoff, Beth Ann. *Why Don't Your Eyelashes Grow? Curious Questions Kids Ask About the Human Body.* New York: Avery, 2008.

Macaulay, David. *The Way We Work: Getting to Know the Amazing Human Body.* Boston: Houghton Mifflin, 2008.

Spilsbury, Louise. *Eat Smart: A Balanced Diet.* Chicago: Heinemann Library, 2009.

Spilsbury, Louise. *The Human Machine: Digestion and Excretion.* Chicago: Heinemann Library, 2008.

Walker, Richard. *Eyewitness: The Human Body.* New York: Dorling Kindersley, 2009.

Websites

http://dsc.discovery.com/tv/human-body/human-body.html
Find out how far the human body can be pushed. This website has many interesting interactive features as well as quizzes to test your knowledge.

www.mypyramid.gov
This website gives you great advice about what sorts of food and portions you should eat to maintain a healthy body.

http://kidshealth.org/teen/
Find out more about health and your body on this website, which also includes expert answers to common questions.

http://learn.genetics.utah.edu/content/begin/cells/scale
Visit this website to compare the sizes of a human egg, sperm, body cells, bacteria, flu virus, an antibody, and much more!

Topics to research

- Find some of the latest records for human endurance, showing the extremes the body can reach. Here are some ideas to get you started:
  - fastest speed
  - most marathons run
  - swimming speed records
  - survival stories
  - amazing brain and memory feats.

- Investigate the mysteries of body and mind by finding out more about:
  - sleep research
  - how puberty affects moods
  - how exercise can help mental health problems
  - what happens when people sleepwalk.

- Do you want to learn more about the bacteria that live on our bodies? Research the differences between good bacteria and bad bacteria.

Did you know...?

The plastic headphones people wear on airplanes create a warm, moist environment inside the ear where bacteria can breed. Wearing these headphones for just one hour will increase the bacteria in your ear 700 times. This is also worth remembering when you use or share MP3 earphones or cell phones.

Most people can hold their breath for up to one minute when resting. Would you believe the world record for holding the breath is 21 minutes, 29 seconds? In 2009 David Merlini, an escape artist, was lowered into a glass tank of water in front of a large crowd. . . .

"As the seconds moved past the 20:39 minutes mark the spectators started to clap and there was a breathtaking wave of applause when Merlini finally emerged from the tank after 21 minutes and 29 seconds."

Index